The Weather

Written by Olivia George
Illustrated by Rusty Fletcher

children's press®

A Division of Scholastic Inc.
New York Toronto London Auckland Sydney
Mexico City New Delhi Hong Kong
Danbury, Connecticut

Library of Congress Cataloging-in-Publication Data

George, Olivia.
The weather / by Olivia George ; illustrated by Rusty Fletcher.
p. cm. — (My first reader)
Summary: By observing a tree outside the bedroom window, a child is able tell what the weather is like throughout the year.
ISBN 0-516-24880-4 (lib. bdg.) 0-516-24968-1 (pbk.)
[1. Weather—Fiction. 2. Trees—Fiction.] I. Fletcher, Rusty, ill. II. Title. III. Series.
PZ7.G29336We 2005
[E]—dc22
2005004023

Published in 2005 by Children's Press, an imprint of Scholastic Library Publishing.
Published simultaneously in Canada.
Printed in the United States of America.

1 2 3 4 5 6 7 8 9 10 R 14 13 12 11 10 09 08 07 06 05

Note to Parents and Teachers

Once a reader can recognize and identify the 47 words used to tell this story, he or she will be able to successfully read the entire book. These 47 words are repeated throughout the story, so that young readers will be able to recognize the words easily and understand their meaning.

The 47 words used in this book are:

a	gets	it	shade	to
and	getting	leaves	sit	tree
big	green	lemonade	some	warm
branches	ground	move	soon	weather
buds	grow	my	start	wet
cold	has	no	storm	will
comes	have	now	sun	windy
days	I	oh	the	
drink	in	out	then	
fall	is	rainy	there	

Some days it is cold.

My tree has no leaves.

Some days it is windy.

The tree branches move.

Some days it is rainy.

My tree gets wet.

Oh, no! There is a big storm.

Some branches fall to the ground.

The sun comes out.

The weather is getting warm now.

The buds start to grow!

Soon my tree will
have green leaves.

Then I will drink lemonade

and sit in the shade.

ABOUT THE AUTHOR

Olivia George was born and raised in a "children's book family" in Brooklyn, New York, and continues to carry on this tradition from her current home in Oakland, California. Olivia loves all types of weather. *My Tree* is her third book with Nancy Hall.

ABOUT THE ILLUSTRATOR

Rusty Fletcher's childhood dream was to someday be a children's book illustrator. Since 1994, Rusty has been lucky enough to live that dream, creating artwork for children's books, magazines, and greeting cards. Rusty lives in Granville, Ohio, with his wife, Julie, and their two sons, Will and Sam.